THEORETICAL APPROACHES TO DEALING WITH SOMALIA

Abstract

Theoretical approaches to dealing with Somalia by MAJ John G. Gibson, US Army, 47 pages.

Current conditions in Somalia create difficult challenges for the United States. To address ungoverned spaces in the failed state of Somalia, the United States appears to seek multilateral solutions to piracy in the Gulf of Aden, and displays an unwillingness to militarily intervene in Somalia. The United States currently relies on a neo-liberal strategy of limited coalition, international organization, and multilateral agreements to combat piracy of the coast of Somalia, support political development of the Transitional Federal Government of Somalia, and mitigate the effects of famine. Increasingly piracy, famine, and fragile governance plague an already unstable region. Catastrophic conditions exist for the continued exportation of failed state symptoms to Kenya and Ethiopia. US foreign policy and international actions in and around Somalia are too weak to change the current trends of failure. International actors provide critical assistance in funds and food that, no doubt, help reduce suffering. Yet, nothing seems to put an end to the reoccurring theme of crisis and instability.

Seth Kaplan and Bronwyn Bruton, both experts on Somalia, agree that United States policy must change; however, they differ upon the application of new policy. Kaplan offers an intrusive and comprehensive nation building approach while Bruton recommends a policy of constructive disengagement.

The purpose of this essay is to determine if US national interest intersect with the situation in Somalia enough to warrant a change in American foreign policy. Realism and liberalism provide useful tools for examining state actions in the international system. Theories and authors assist policy makers by providing tools for thought and action. Regardless of the tools, Somalia continues to prove a difficult problem. It is the hypothesis of this essay that the United States should constructively disengage from Somalia, while providing a roadmap for international recognition for Somaliland, and simultaneously begin deliberate nation building in Kenya, Ethiopia, Eritrea, and Djibouti.

TABLE OF CONTENTS

CHAPTER 1

INTRODUCTION

Context and Orientation

In 1878, the German philosopher Friederich Nietzsche critiqued more than just human nature when he said, "[c]onvictions are more dangerous enemies of truth than lies."[1] Convictions create powerful engines of human action. Convictions, even if false, direct behavior. Nietzsche's statement defines the danger of blindly following conviction. Therefore, conviction can also be illusion. Through Nietzsche's lens, human narratives possess conviction and illusion and depend upon the human construction of context for meaning. Nietzsche created a paradox between conviction and illusion with truth left to the minds of men.

In 1952, political scientist William Brogan commented that the United States suffered from an illusion of omnipotence.[2] Presidential historian Robert Dalleck combines Nietzsche's conviction with Brogan's observations to create a discussion about the invisible tyranny of metaphor upon American foreign policy.[3] Dallek argues that universalism, distaste for appeasement, and belief in the effectiveness of military strength trap American thinking about foreign policy problems. Dallek states that the three myths, or illusions, tyrannize American presidents with limited tools for foreign policy solutions.

William Brogan's article contrasts the victorious America of 1945 against the frustrated context of 1952. American politicians were frustrated with the stalemate in North Korea against a supposed

---

[1] Friedrich Wilhelm Nietzsche, *Human, All Too Human : A Book for Free Spirits* (Lincoln: University of Nebraska Press, 1984), 483. Nietzsche believed that man interpreted his own truth through perceptivism (creating his own reality). Nietzsche's aphorism also discusses the possibility that no truth actually exists but that which man assigns.

[2] William Brogan, "The Illusion of American Omnipotence," *Harper's Magazine* December 1952, 1-2,6. Brogan discusses the problem of an American idea that all international actions in the world are in some way the result of American action or inaction.

[3] Robert Dallek, "The Tyranny of Metaphor," *Foreign Policy* 182, (2010). Dallek uses the tyranny of metaphor to describe how American Presidents serve as prisoners of metaphor instead of shapers of history.

inferior China and North Korea. Brogan thought that Americans failed to appreciate the self-determination of other peoples, in light of their own. Brogan argues that to Americans, in 1952, any situation that distresses or endangers the United States can only exist because some other Americans were either fools or knaves.[4]

Brogan supposes that America is not omnipotent and that global American hegemony is an illusion, not universally expected or desired. Brogan's case for the illusion of omnipotence centers on the American perception about the Chinese Revolution. For Brogan, in spite of historical context, the Chinese Revolution, an event of immense importance, is often discussed as if it were simply some problem in American foreign and domestic policy and politics.[5] Further, he identifies the larger context of the Chinese Revolution in the historical narrative of the Chinese people, who once viewed themselves as earth's Middle Kingdom.[6] William Brogan ends his argument by stating that American ideas of democracy, equality, and the courage to fight for others represent true power. He concludes with a statement that sadly Americans are not omnipotent. However, "only by accepting this depressing truth can American power, great, flexible, and beneficent as it is, be used to full advantage."[7]

Through Brogan and Nietzsche's narrative, Robert Dallek frames the three illusions in American foreign policy over the last 100 years.[8] First, Dallek addresses American universalism similar to Walter

---

[4] Brogan, 1.

[5] Ibid., 3.

[6] Ibid., 3-7. Brogan discusses flawed thinking in America. The Chinese Revolution affected the oldest civilization on planet earth. He cites that the revolution affects 1/5th of the human population. Brogan argues that the Chinese Revolution had deep Chinese roots, only apparent to Chinese people. Brogan then uses American blame for the Chinese Revolution against General Marshall, Secretary Acheson, and President Roosevelt as evidence of this illusion. The Middle Kingdom refers to the Chinese cultural view that they are the center of the earth. The word China translates to middle kingdom or central nation; Geoff Wade, *The Polity of Yelang and the Origin of the Name "China"*, Sino-Platonic Papers, vol. No. 188, 6.

[7] Brogan, 8.

[8] Dallek., 2-5. Dallek chronicles the high water marks for American foreign policy from President Wodrow Wilson to George W. Bush. He champions the American success in WW II, Truman Doctrine, Marshall Plan, diplomacy in the Cuban Missile Crisis, the Camp David peace accords, the opening of China, detente with the

McDougall's global meliorism.[9] Brogan and Dallek recognize the power of vision, but not in the American tendency to think that the peoples of the world await their share of the American dream. The danger of universalism lies in seeing the world as a place for Americans to fix. Dallek places the roots of universalism in President Woodrow Wilson's fourteen points. He argues that Wilsonianism found life after World War II in the triumph of democracy in creation of the United Nations. However, just as Wilson's fourteen points could not stop the First World War, the United Nations did little to stop the Cold War. Dallek illustrates, like McDougall, that America will never cure countries of an affinity for bloodshed.

Robert Dallek connects the universalism illusion to the present conflicts in Iraq and Afghanistan. Conviction mixed with universalism explains President Bush's rational for fighting in Iraq. Dallek calls President Bush's prediction that the destruction of Saddam Hussein's military dictatorship as the first step of transforming the Middle East into liberal democracies as elusive as President Wilson's vision in 1918.[10] Dallek submits that the results of 10 years of war for Iraq and Afghanistan point to an unpredictable future at best. He states that with 10, 20, or 30 years of stewardship, both Iraq and Afghanistan may shape up. Yet, the American people will not endure such expenditure of blood and treasure. The American people and the memories of Vietnam prevent such extended care taking in far off lands. The second illusion firmly rests near the memory of the Vietnam War in the American tradition.

Dallek states the second illusion trapping American foreign policy thinking is a complete denial of the concept of compromise. The concept of compromise, any type, is tantamount to defeat in the American narrative. For Dallek, Neville Chamberlain's appeasement of Hitler in Munich of 1938, casts a

---

Soviet Union, and the Panama Canal Treaty as significant accomplishments. He argues that a more holistic view would include misfortunes.

[9] Walter A. McDougall, *Promised Land, Crusader State : The American Encounter with the World since 1776* (Boston: Houghton Mifflin, 1997), 172-198.

[10] Dallek: 4. Dallek quotes President Bush to demonstrate the universalism and connection to President Wilson. "The survival of liberty in our land increasingly depends on the success of liberty in other lands. The best hope for peace in our world is the expansion of freedom in all the world."

long shadow over American foreign policy. Dallek argues that for American's it is always 1938, no matter whether dealing with Saddam Hussein, Slobodan Milosevic, or "Baby Doc" Duvalier.[11] The word appeasement immediately spells defeat for the American psyche. Yet, appeasement has its place in all policy, according to Winston Churchill. Compromise represents the essence of diplomacy and yet the legacy of Munich casts a disheartening shadow over American foreign policy. Dallek argues that universalism combined with no room for compromise led America into costly and unwise military adventures. Dallek places the advance of American forces above the 38th Parallel during the Korean War and President Johnson's escalation of Vietnam as misadventures caused by the first two illusions.

Dallek's third illusion stems from the first two. Robert Dallek argues that American presidents often hold militarized containment as the only way to avoid the first two traps. Containment policy and the Cold War rested heavily on the use of military power to back the strategic economic, political, and information objectives designed to collapse the Soviet Union. However, George Kennan never wanted National Security Council (NSC) 68.[12] The heavy reliance on military power to accomplish foreign policy goals creates weak strategies for diplomatic, political, and economic development. According to Dallek, Presidents Eisenhower and Kennedy's actions can teach future presidents about the benefits of limiting military force in foreign policy.[13]

Rober Dallek identifies three illusions that provide context for the current American foreign policy discourse. Dallek's illusions remain powerful engines of influence upon the American narrative.

---

[11] Ibid.

[12] Ibid., 5. In later years, George Kennan regretted the adoption of his ideas into a strategy. He believed that economic competition could destroy communism from within, not military containment. Kennan eventually saw the problem as a political and economic struggle, not a military one. Moreover, Kennan opposed the invasion of Iraq, calling a great mistake.

[13] Ibid. Dallek argues that President Eisenhower limited military involvement for the United States by not attacking Pyongyang in 1952, resisting the calls from Hungary (1956) and France (Dien Ben Phu, 1953) for direct long term military assistance. He argues that President Kennedy resisted the tendency to escalate the Cuban Missile Crisis, the Bay of Pigs, and possibly Vietnam. Dallek states that the history of Johnson's presidency vindicates Kennedy's doubts about Vietnam.

Most importantly, American illusions of omnipotence combined with the tyranny of metaphor explain the orientation of American approaches to foreign policy. Nietzsche's aphorism explains that American foreign policy makers sometimes fail to see actions in the light of reality because of conviction, illusion, metaphor, or all three.

Illusion, conviction, and myth abound for United States aims in East Africa. Somalia is routinely called the dark crystal of failed states. The Foreign Policy Failed States Index, fed by The Fund For Peace, shows Somalia as the world's number one failed state since 2008. Not only do the indicators point to Somalia to remain on the path of failure, it already has failed.[14] Should US foreign policy continue along the same course, trapped by the same tyrannies, Somalis will continue to suffer, and so will East Africa.

The current security narrative focuses primarily on Operation Enduring Freedom, while other efforts require serious attention, if not completely new approaches. American policy may not change the fate of Somalia; however, US policy reform could put regional partners, such as Kenya, Ethiopia, Eritrea, and Djibouti, on a path to improved security, substantial counterterrorist capabilities, and new economic development. The current policy seems to suffer Brogan's illusion and each of Dallek's myths. East Africa is a dismal place and will continue to frustrate the international community for the near future.

---

[14] Fund For Peace, 2012. "The Failed State Index," http://www.fundforpeace.org/global/?q=fsi-grid2008.

CHAPTER 2

RESEARCH METHODOLOGY

United States foreign policy towards Somalia needs reform. This essay compares and contrasts two relevant approaches to dealing with Somalia and evaluates their value against the elements of operational art and current conditions. Using the existing ideological narrative between realism and liberalism, this essay examines the relevant context of both the liberal and realist tradition with respect to the present situation in Somalia. Seth Kaplan, a fragile state development expert, and Bronwyn Bruton, a Council on Foreign Relations Fellow and Somalia expert, provide contrasting recommendations for Somalia. Using a case study, the paper examines the effectiveness of United States counter-piracy operations off the coast of Somalia to illuminate challenges in the current environment. Then, using Kaplan and Bruton's hypothetical approaches, determine which recommendation is best if implemented by the United States. The author then evaluates each approach against the elements of operational art.[15]

Current conditions in Somalia create difficult challenges for the United States. To address ungoverned spaces in the failed state of Somalia, the United States appears to seek multilateral solutions to piracy in the Gulf of Aden, and displays an unwillingness to militarily intervene in Somalia. The United States currently relies on a neo-liberal strategy of limited coalition, international organization, and multilateral agreements to combat piracy of the coast of Somalia, support political development of the Transitional Federal Government of Somalia, and mitigate the effects of famine. Increasingly piracy, famine, and fragile governance plague an already unstable region. Catastrophic conditions exist for the continued exportation of failed state symptoms to Kenya and Ethiopia. US foreign policy and

---

[15] The elements of operational art include the following: end state and conditions, centers of gravity, direct or indirect approach, logical lines of operations or effort, operational reach, tempo, simultaneity and depth, phasing and transitions, culmination, and risk.

international actions in and around Somalia are too weak to change the current trends of failure. International actors provide critical assistance in funds and food that, no doubt, help reduce suffering. Yet, nothing seems to put an end to the reoccurring theme of crisis and instability.

Seth Kaplan and Bronwyn Bruton, both experts on Somalia, agree that United States policy must change; however, they differ upon the application of new policy. Kaplan offers an intrusive and comprehensive nation building approach while Bruton recommends a policy of constructive disengagement.

The purpose of this essay is to determine if US national interest intersect with the situation in Somalia enough to warrant a change in American foreign policy. Realism and liberalism provide useful tools for examining state actions in the international system. Theories and authors assist policy makers by providing tools for thought and action. Regardless of the tools, Somalia continues to prove a difficult problem. It is the hypothesis of this essay that the United States should constructively disengage from Somalia, while providing a roadmap for international recognition for Somaliland, and simultaneously begin deliberate nation building in Kenya, Ethiopia, Eritrea, and Djibouti.

CHAPTER 3

LITERATURE REVIEW

The Current United States Response to Piracy in The Gulf of Aden: The Need for a New Policy

Liberal theory of international relations best explains the current United States efforts to combat the threat of piracy in the Gulf of Aden. Liberal theory illuminates cooperation as the critical aspect of current United States efforts to project order in a troubled section of the global commons. United States foreign policy towards piracy in the Gulf of Aden and Somalia consists of the United States Countering Piracy Off the Horn of Africa: Partnership and Action Plan.[16] The United States participates in the United Nations multilateral efforts consisting of Naval Task Force operations, the Contact Group on Piracy off the Coast of Somalia, and the Djibouti Code of Conduct to address the environment in Somalia and the Gulf of Aden.

Neo-liberalism or structural liberalism, defined by Charles Kegley, is the "new" liberal theoretical perspective that accounts for the way international institutions promote global change, cooperation, peace, and prosperity through collective programs for reform.[17] Regardless of the Neo distraction, the theory is still liberalism. The key component of liberal theory is that it recognizes the importance of non-state actors and cooperation for security. Neo-liberalism endorses collective security and cooperation, through organizations such as the North Atlantic Treaty Organization or the United Nations, over unilateral action.

---

[16] National Security Council, US, *Countering Piracy Off the Coast of Africa: Partnership Action Plan* December 2008. Annex B, 15-17. Annex B, 15-17. Actual document describes the official policy of the United States of America to combat piracy.

[17] Charles W. Kegley and Shannon Lindsey Blanton, *World Politics : Trend and Transformation*, 12th ed. (Australia ; Boston: Wadsworth Cengage Learning, 2010), 36. Charles Kegley currently serves as a permanent board member for the Carnige Council on Foreign Relations. He published forty-seven books about American foreign policy and international relations. Charles Kegley continues to publish the World Politics book as a student text. The current text is the 12th edition.

Joseph Nye further defines neo-liberalism as having four distinct components that help shape actors and actions in the international system. Neo-liberalist institutions provide continuity, opportunity for reciprocity, flow of information, and methods for conflict resolutions for state actors.[18] The critical portion of understanding the link between liberalist theory and the current environment is the use of the institution, specifically the Uited Nations, to reduce anarchy in the system. The United States, African countries, North Atlantic Treaty Organization members, Russia, China, and India operate together, with United Nations support, to secure the Gulf of Aden, protect the Global Commons, and counter piracy.

According to the United States Department of Transportation, Maritime Administration, in 2009, the economic impact of piracy was approximately 89 million dollars to avoid the Gulf of Aden by traversing the Cape of Good Hope (per maritime carrier).[19] The price of avoidance increases with reduced efficiency, extra fuel, increased insurance, and additional ships to account for the 2,700-mile addition to the shipping route.[20] The United Nations, North Atlantic Treaty Organization, African Union, United States, Russia, China, and India all participate in naval operations to counter piracy in the Gulf of Aden. The United Nations serves as the lead global institution for piracy legislation. The latest United Nations resolution, resolution 1950, passed in 2010, addresses how to deal with pirates at sea and on land in Somalia. The resolution states that nations can participate in any capacity needed to defend shipping interest while acting in self-defense. The resolution also states that nations must prosecute pirates in legitimate courts of law. Kenya and Seychelles currently represent the only African countries prosecuting captured pirates in Africa.[21] The international system struggles to stop piracy and enforce the rule of law

---

[18] Joseph S. Nye, *Understanding International Conflicts : An Introduction to Theory and History*, 7th ed., Longman Classics in Political Science (New York: Pearson Longman, 2009), 60.

[19] *Economic Impact of Piracy in the Gulf of Aden on Global Trade*December 02, 2010. http://www.marad.dot.gov/documents/HOA_Economic%20Impact%20of%20Piracy.pdf

[20] Ibid., 1.

[21] Bridget Coggins, "The Pirate Den," *Foreign Policy*, no. July/August (2010). http://www.foreignpolicy.com/articles/2010/06/21/prime_numbers

in the Gulf of Aden. Piracy off the coast of Somalia significantly influences the security of the Global Commons and the United Nations encourages more cooperation between international and regional powers to combat the problem.

The United Nations currently leads the international effort to combat piracy in the Gulf of Aden with the Transitional Federal Government of Somalia. The United Nations leads the naval effort, Combined Maritime Forces Combined Task Force-151, to secure the Gulf of Aden, but land-based solutions in Somalia are in short supply. The United Nations facilitated the establishment of the Contact Group on Piracy off the Coast of Somalia (CGPCS) in January of 2009.[22] The Contact Group on Piracy off the Coast of Somalia has fifty-three member countries and four working group initiatives as of June 2010. The Contact Group on Piracy off the Coast of Somalia formed the working groups to take action against piracy and to provide the Transitional Federal Government of Somalia with tools for security assistance.[23] Working group one, chaired by the United Kingdom, focuses on naval interdiction and disruption of pirate activities. Working group two, chaired by Denmark, focuses on the international law pertaining to prosecution of pirates through legitimate court systems. Working group three, chaired by the United States, focuses on the development of counter-pirate capabilities within the shipping industry. Working group four, chaired by Egypt, seeks to improve diplomatic and public information efforts against all aspects of piracy. The Contact Group on Piracy off the Coast of Somalia serves an excellent example of a neo-liberalist approach to combating piracy in the Gulf of Aden.

The United Nations facilitated the creation of the Djibouti Code of Conduct, a regional cooperation agreement aimed at combating piracy through sharing information, joint interdiction, and cooperative prosecution of pirates.[24] The United Nations also assisted in creating a trust fund for member

---

[22] *Report to the Secretary-General Pursuant to Security Council Resolution 1897 (2009)* October 27, 2010. 4-5. http://daccess-dds-ny.un.org/doc/UNDOC/GEN/N10/588/02/PDF/N1058802.pdf

[23] Ibid.

[24] Ibid.

states called the Djibouti Code Trust Fund, which allows the International Maritime Organization to coordinate and manage member activities. The International Maritime Organization also created a regional training initiative focused on law enforcement, command and control, and maritime operations for member states of the Djibouti Code of Conduct.

The United Nations sponsored the creation of three naval task force elements designated to enforce security in the Gulf of Aden. The European Union (European Union Naval Force- Operation Atlanta), Combined Maritime Forces Combined Task Force-151, and North Atlantic Treaty Organization (Operation Ocean Shield) provide escort and security in the Gulf of Aden and logistical support to the African Union Mission in Somalia. United Nations member states also conduct independent naval operations in the area to supplement the United Nations collective efforts.[25] The United Nations used international naval coordination as a foundation to begin ground operations and efforts in Somalia.

The root causes of piracy are land-based and stem from the near failed government of Somalia. The ungoverned spaces in Somalia allow piracy, crime, and terrorist groups to prosper. The United States, African Union Mission in Somalia, and the United Nations recognize the importance of fixing more than just piracy.[26] On 27 October 2010, in a report to the United Nations Security Council, Secretary General Ban Ki-moon confirmed that piracy is a symptom of weak governance in Somalia.[27] Maritime operations continue to take place, but Somalia requires more United States or United Nations support to provide capacity for security.

Neo-liberal, or structural liberalism best explains the current international response to piracy in the Gulf of Aden and off the coast of Somalia. International cooperation and coordination must increase as the security situation degrades. The United Nations remains the lead institution for coordinating concerned state efforts. Regional, international, and independent state actors, in conjunction with Non-

---

[25] Ibid., 6.

[26] US, *Countering Piracy Off the Coast of Africa: Partnership Action Plan*, 6.

[27] United Nations, 14.

Governmental Organization, and other relief efforts must address the situation in Somalia to prevent regional disorder. In April 2010, pirates conducted the most daring heist to date, "sailing some 1,200 nautical miles from the Somali coast -- right past the naval task forces led by the United States, European Union, and the North Atlantic Treaty Organization, as well as the independently commanded Chinese, Russian, and Indian flotillas -- to seize three Thai fishing boats along with their 77 crewmembers. In terms of distance offshore and sheer number of hostages taken, the raid broke all previous records."[28] The levels of international coordination must increase to stabilize Somalia, because no actor is able to fix the environment independently.

The ungoverned space of Somalia, piracy and crime, mixed with drugs and terrorism present the global community with a difficult problem. The above analysis describes how countries act in neo-liberal ways to combat piracy off the coast of Somalia, improve governance in Somalia, and protect a global shipping lane. Significant contributions by the United States towards the international effort, to deter piracy are important; however, the United States does not act unilaterally. No one else in Somalia does either. American foreign policy, stated in the United States Maritime Security (Piracy) Policy, provides a detailed plan for multilateralism, diplomatic, military, economic, intelligence, law enforcement, and judicial action.[29] Yet, the policy is ambiguous in action. The policy does provide broad concept mission orders to the agencies and departments of the United States Government for dealing with piracy related issues. The indirect nature of the policy does provide the United States a wide spectrum of options for working initiatives through the United Nations. The United States State Department led efforts within the United Nations to create the Contact Group on Piracy off the Coast of Somalia, the Djibouti Code of

---

[28] Peter J. Pham, "Lawyers Vs. Pirates," *Foreign Policy*, (April 30, 2010).

[29] US, *Countering Piracy Off the Coast of Africa: Partnership Action Plan*, 15-16.

Conduct, Djibouti Trust Fund, and the European Union, North Atlantic Treaty Organization, Combined Maritime Forces Combined Task Force-151 Naval Task Force elements.[30]

Ultimately, the United States seeks a multilateral solution to piracy off the coast of Somalia, and further ashore to address ungoverned spaces in the near failed state of Somalia. United States unwillingness to go ashore in Somalia, places the bulk of American effort in the neo-liberal category of using coalition, international organizations, and multilateral agreements to combat piracy off the coast of Somalia. The recommendations of Lauren Ploch from Congressional Research Service, and Bronwyn Bruton, of the Council on Foreign Relations, share Vice Admiral William Gortney's, Commander, United States Naval Forces Central Command, assessment to the House Armed Service Committee on 05 March 2009 in which he stated, "[u]ltimately piracy is a problem that starts ashore and requires an international solution ashore. We made this clear at the offset of our efforts. We can not guarantee safety in this vast region."[31] The Admiral is right. The actions of the United States, as well as other relevant global actors, demonstrate an inability or unwillingness to fix Somalia or rid the Gulf of Aden of piracy.

The failed country and piracy policy prompted scholars to develop new approaches to deal with Somalia. The two most prominent proposals come from Seth Kaplan and Bronwyn Bruton. Seth Kaplan offers a modern Liberalist solution while Bruton proposes a more traditional Realist stance. The two approaches share common ground in the Realist and Liberalist theories of international relations.

Significant Ideological Narratives

Navigation through the waters surrounding the Horn of Africa, specifically, near Somalia, proves difficult even for the most powerful naval power in the world. Somalia produces piracy, failed government, limited international intervention, famine, and terrorism. United States foreign policy

---

[30] Congressional Research Service, *Piracy Off the Horn of Africa* September 28, 2009. 16-21.

[31] Bronwyn Burton, "Disengaging from Somalia, Interview by Deborah Jerome," *Council on Foreign Relations*, (March 10, 2010); Ploch, 35.

discourse towards Somalia proves just as complicated to navigate as the waters themselves. Competing narratives concerning the best practices in security policy, post-9/11, conflicting international relations theories, and changing political environments create a difficult situation for identifying clear policy approaches for dealing with Somalia.

To evaluate American foreign policy in Somalia, one must understand the convictions, illusions, and tyrannous myths at play in American policy today. The American tradition grows from both realist and liberalist thought. The detailed history of American foreign policy truths and traditions is simply beyond the scope of this paper. However, one must understand that, like any state actor in the Westphalian system, the state contorts between serving two masters: her interests and her values. Though a rational person desires clear delineation and classification of American actions with respect to foreign policy responses, this is simply not possible.

Classic realist theorists and authors span from Thucydides to Stephen Waltz.[32] Realist theory rests on observations about man and government. Realists view war and the use of force to protect interests as the major problem of international relations.[33] Realists see states as the primary actors. To compare, liberal thought maintains some of the Realist foundations, like anarchy in international relations for example, but adds some notable differences. Liberals see other actors as equal or primary to the state. Liberals envision a global society that functions in parallel with states.[34] Liberal theory places value on collective security and individual rights as major outcomes of state policy. Realists may cooperate and champion human rights, but only for calculated self-interest and short-term gain.

---

[32] Kenneth Neal Waltz, *Man, the State, and War; a Theoretical Analysis*, Topical Studies in International Relations (New York,: Columbia University Press, 1959). Waltz is considered the leading neo-realist theorist. He wrote this book in 1959 and brought neo-realism to the forefront of international politics debates.

[33] Joseph S. Nye, David Welch, and Joseph S. Nye, *Understanding Global Conflict and Cooperation : An Introduction to Theory and History*, 8th ed. (Boston: Pearson Longman, 2011).4-5. Joseph Nye outlines the major currents of international relations theory. He provides context into the different historical traditions of realist and liberal. Nye places the issue of anarchy as the center issue that schools of thought view differently. Therefore, according to Nye, it is the state response to anarchy that defines actions as realist or liberalist.

[34] Ibid., 4-5. Joseph Nye provides an excellent capture of the conversation between realists and liberals.

17

Regardless of the international relations theory, individuals and thus states, organize, cooperate, and war around the central idea of managing uncertainty (anarchy) while balancing the tension between fear, honor, and interest with respect to other individuals, and states within the international system. Realism and liberalism define thoughts into theory in an attempt to explain human actions, predict policy, and explain behavior. Yet, human behaviors do not exactly follow models. Realism and Liberalism both attempt to deal with how people and countries self-organize, act, and react with respect to uncertainty in the international system. Therefore, the setting for the unfolding narrative of human, state, and collective interaction defines itself in terms of management of anarchy, uncertainty, or fear.[35] The Athenian writer, Thucydides, captures human interaction in his history of the Peloponnesian War, by characterizing human interaction driven by fear, honor, and interest.[36] Joseph Nye Jr. and Kenneth N. Waltz stand apart in the current theoretical context for dealing with international conflict and 21st century security concerns.[37]

Context of Current Liberal Narrative

Joseph Nye, a prominent American liberal theorist, delivers American liberalist ideas with a realist vocabulary.[38] As the primary advocate and author of the soft power or whole of government

---

[35] John J. Mearsheimer, *The Tragedy of Great Power Politics* (New York: Norton, 2001), 9. Mearsheimer argues that anarchy is the impetus for state organization. Hedging against anarchy is the organizing principle of international systems.

[36] Thucydides, *The Landmark Thucydides : A Comprehensive Guide to the Peloponnesian War*, Newly rev. ed. (New York: Simon & Schuster, 1998), 351-357. The Melian Dialogue presents the classic realist idea that the strong do what they can and the weak suffer what they must.

[37] Seth D. Kaplan, *Fixing Fragile States : A New Paradigm for Development* (Westport, Conn.: Praeger Security International, 2008). Introduction, Seth Kaplan discusses literature and thought about causes for fragile or failed states. Kaplan's book recommends a nuanced approach, locally and culturally driven for true progress in a failed state.

[38] In addition to publishing *The Paradox of American Power*, *Bound to Lead*, *Soft Power*, and *Understanding Global Conflict and Cooperation*, Joseph Nye was the dean of the Kennedy School of Government at Harvard University, Chairman of the National Intelligence Council, and an Assistant Secretary of Defense.

approach, Joseph Nye stands out from present day international relations theorists by advocating for overmatched American military power, coupled with soft power.[39]

Nye coined both soft power and smart power as the terms used today to describe the current and future United States foreign policy strategy.[40] He envisions a world that cannot survive without the United States, as well as a United States that cannot survive without the world. Nye's vision describes the classic liberalist view of international relations. Liberalism is simply realism with a different view about primary actors and human nature. Liberals view non-state actors, churches, diaspora, or multi-national corporations as relevant actors in the international system. Liberalists also believe that individual relationships and human ethics mitigate anarchy in the international system.[41] The interesting part of Joseph Nye's argument for soft power lies in his delivery. Nye uses realist terms to define power relationships for the 21st century.

Joseph Nye creates a convincing argument that leadership and moral superiority provide the cheapest way to achieve desired national strategic outcomes. Nye outlines the use of soft power in current power politics to pressure and ease the divisive nature of many issues. For example, the United States co-opted 60 years of alliances from the soft power wielded through the Marshall Plan after World War II.[42] However, after the attacks on September 11, 2001, the United States generally acted unilaterally in both Afghanistan and Iraq. Nye argues that American moral force suffered. He posits that the new war against terror helps smooth over some the rough edges of American actions, but not enough. The fear of terrorism

---

[39] Joseph S. Nye, *Soft Power : The Means to Success in World Politics*, 1st ed. (New York: Public Affairs, 2004).

[40] Joseph S. Nye, "Get Smart," *Foreign Affairs* 88, no. 4 (Jul/Aug 2009). Nye developed the term Smart Power in 2003 to counter the misunderstanding to his previous term soft power. Hilary Clinton used the term smart power in her Secretary of State confirmation hearing. Joseph Nye defines smart power as the calculated combination of soft and hard power.

[41] Nye, *Soft Power : The Means to Success in World Politics*. 8. The table on page 8 describes the tension between soft and hard power and the associated motivators for behavioral change. The chart outlines the idea that leadership leads others to achieve your goals with out losing credibility through coercion or bribery.

[42] Ibid., 129.

may not provide enough fear for other nations to tolerate the United States. Nye argues that if support for the United States becomes so un-popular in a country, that being pro-American is the domestic kiss of death, political leaders will become unlikely to make concessions.[43] Joseph Nye presents the opportunity cost of arrogance in hard power approaches.

The future of American power, according to Nye, lies in humility and focus. Humility by the United States to leverage the moral power of liberal ideas such as freedom, democracy, and human rights, while remaining focused on global leadership. He specifically warns against the seduction of empire. Nye uses the example of American empire to describe the vulnerability of open western cultures to extremist threats. Moreover, Nye warns against forceful control in the international system. He states that many pundits like to argue for hard power protection of American interests abroad. Joseph Nye characterizes this thinking as a foreign policy disaster.[44] Hard power cannot provide the solutions for understanding and coping with the 21st century global information age.[45]

Joseph Nye delivers his most convincing argument by describing the importance of soft power during the Cold War. He demonstrates that military force clearly kept a balance of power and contained the expansion of the Union of Soviet Socialist Republics. Yet, that military force never actually fought against the Soviet Union. American soft power fought, infiltrated, disrupted, and ultimately won the Cold War.[46] Nye counsels American policy makers that military force and power are critical, yet not the most effective tool in securing American prosperity in the future. Everett Dolman defines strategy in the space and information age, Nye's 21st century global information age, as a continuum of creating conditions of

---

[43] Ibid., 129.

[44] Ibid., 136-139. Nye clearly states that the connotations of empire, imperialism, and global domination create unrealistic expectations, international fear, and ultimately undermine the true strength of the United States, soft power.

[45] Ibid., 139.

[46] Ibid., 142, 147. Nye states that the United States demonstrated an excellent understanding of soft power resources and implementation during the Cold War.

advantage to secure a better future, not explicitly "winning."[47] Joseph Nye sees a future with deeper

understanding of American soft power and its utility in letting others win to help the United States

strategic outcomes, all the while balancing soft and hard power in foreign policy.

Context of Realist Narrative.

Kenneth N. Waltz offers a different view of world politics and human interaction. Waltz wrote

Man, The State, and War as a way to describe how humans, states, and systems react to anarchy and each

other.[48] Waltz personally describes his work as an attempt to illuminate predictive patterns of human,

state, and thus system interaction to better understand war and international relations.[49] Kenneth Waltz

argued that international politics represents human desire to exert control over anarchy and uncertainty.

Waltz went on to write the book *Theory of International Politics* to present his theory of international

relations.[50] According to Waltz, states take action in response to the anarchic nature of the international

system.[51] Therefore, states act in response to the anarchic nature of the international system of politics.

Kenneth Waltz created the idea of neo-realism.

Kenneth Waltz insight and theory created a new method for understanding state actions in

response to uncertainty. Neo-realism provides a lens to examine the changes in the global environment

after World War II. Waltz catalogues the progression of realist thought starting with Thucydides,

followed by Machiavelli, Thomas Hobbes, and Hans Morgenthau.[52] Neo-realist theory critically

---

[47] Everett C. Dolman, *Pure Strategy : Power and Principle in the Space and Information Age*, Cass Series-- Strategy and History (London ; New York: Frank Cass, 2005). 3-6.

[48] Waltz., 159.

[49] P Schouten, "Theory Talk #40: Kenneth Waltz- the Physiocrat of Internatinal Politcs'," *Theory Talks*, (2011). Kenneth Waltz

[50] Kenneth Neal Waltz, *Theory of International Politics*, Addison-Wesley Series in Political Science (Reading, Mass.: Addison-Wesley Pub. Co., 1979).

[51] Schouten. Waltz discusses the importance of developing connections between the most important variables in the international system.

[52] Ibid.

illuminates United States actions during the Cold War, and illuminates policy direction post-9/11. Neo-realist theory explains American expansion after the fall of the Soviet Union. The theory also addresses the underlying theme behind the most recent American Global War on Terror. The United States fits a pattern of expansion after surprise. American safety comes from expansion, rather than contracting, in international politics.[53] Waltz's ideas of neo-realism saturate the current discourse, between nations, of international politics.

Kenneth Waltz identified anarchy as the organizing principle in international politics.[54] He argues that with anarchy as the organizing principle, units or actors, organize accordingly. Waltz's significant connection between *Man, The State, and War* and *Theory of International Politics* is that anarchy defines the system and that states are the highest authority. Therefore, without hierarchical structures, international relations revolve around actors organizing, securing, and dominating the environment, all the while reducing anarchy. Further, Waltz stated that in an environment of self-help, organized to mitigate anarchy, strong units act to secure future prosperity.[55]

After the Cold War and post-9/11, Kenneth Waltz's theory, rests at the center of friction in the global system. According to Kenneth Waltz and Joseph Nye, United States policies shape the global structure of politics and international affairs. However, the authors differ significantly upon the sources of friction, power, and prospect of sustained American power in the 21st century.

In order to integrate international relations theory to the current operational environment, one must examine the unfolding of events in context. Historian, John Lewis Gaddis describes history as a

---

[53] John Lewis Gaddis, *Surprise, Security, and the American Experience*, Joanna Jackson Goldman Memorial Lecture on American Civilization and Government (Cambridge, MA: Harvard University Press, 2004).

[54] Harry Kreisler, "Theory and International Politcs: Conversation with Kenneth N. Waltz," (February 10, 2003).

[55] Thucydides, 352. Reference the Melian Dialogue where Thucydides writes that the strong do as they will and the weak suffer what they must.

narrative of friction between human oppression and freedom.[56] International relations, specifically, the

battle of ideas driving current American foreign policy and strategy, express a similar friction. Gaddis

discusses the tension between oppression and freedom associated with the pursuit of history and its

application to the present. He posits that people are oppressed by the circumstances of the present, while

at the same time emancipated by the ability to struggle for positive outcomes.[57] Gaddis describes the

dialectic nature of human experience as a metaphor for complex examination in history. Gaddis

ultimately argues that humans do not live in a reductionist fashion, so all variables are important. Thus,

historical context gains primacy over variables and narrative. John Lewis Gaddis uses the painting of a

wanderer standing at the top of a rock precipice looking over the edge, into fog, terrain, mountains,

valley, and uncertainty.[58] The uncertainty, perspective, and disposition of the Wanderer, depends upon the

observer's interpretation of the painting.[59] Gaddis and the Wanderer demonstrate the importance of

context in narrative. The contrast and ambiguity aptly capture the uncertainty facing the United States

with respect to the machinations of applying national strategy to secure a better future.[60] Given Waltz and

Nye's ideas, placed over the bedrock ideas of realism and liberalism, one can now appreciate some

aspects of the discourse of American foreign policy. To illuminate possible realities of implementing

policy, one must understand where competing narratives intersect in the discourse.[61]

---

[56] John Lewis Gaddis, *The Landscape of History : How Historians Map the Past* (Oxford ; New York: Oxford University Press, 2002). 147.

[57] Ibid., 147.

[58] Ibid. Gaddis uses the painting to serve as his platform to discuses the tension between the past and future. He argues that history serves only those that are willing to wander.

[59] Ibid., 150.

[60] Dolman., 6.

[61] John A. Lynn, *Battle : A History of Combat and Culture*, Rev. and updated ed. (Cambridge, MA: Westview Press, 2004).

Intrusive Nation-building versus Constructive Disengagement

American foreign policy towards Somalia and the countries of Eastern Africa represent an example of 21st century fault lines between the realist and liberalist traditions. To accurately describe United States policy outcomes in East Africa and Somalia one must view the narrative with respect to the theoretical traditions and Robert Dallek's tyranny of metaphor. American development of limited programs to secure regional stability for economic trade dominates the policy discourse about Eastern Africa. Security, stability, and trade in Somalia present difficult problems for the international community and the United States. Limited intervention coupled with United Nations measures cloud the already muddled issue of international development in Somalia. Seth D. Kaplan and Bronwyn E. Bruton offer differing interpretations of best practices for success in Somalia. Kaplan and Bruton seek to offer new policy options for improving the future of Somalia, and the international community.

Seth D. Kaplan's book, *Fixing Fragile States*, discusses a new approach for developing stability in fragile or failing states. Kaplan presents development as cure for fragile states, but through nuanced development. Kaplan advances that only by re-designing political processes and governance structures to fit within local concepts can legitimacy, rule of law, and other ingredients foster a self-sustaining internally driven process that leads to development.[62] Kaplan's thesis is surprisingly similar to current democratic peace theorist Bruce Russet's assertions about the connection between governance, political culture, and development.[63]

---

[62] Kaplan., Chapter 1, 9.

[63] John R. Oneal Bruce Russett, David R. Davis, "The Third Leg of the Kantian Tripod for Peace: International Organizations and Militarized Disputes, 1950-1985," *International Organization* 52, no. No. 3 (Summer, 1998); Bruce M. Russett, *Grasping the Democratic Peace : Principles for a Post-Cold War World* (Princeton, N.J.: Princeton University Press, 1993); Bruce M. Russett and John R. Oneal, *Triangulating Peace : Democracy, Interdependence, and International Organizations* (New York: Norton, 2001); John R. Oneal and Bruce Russett, "Clear and Clean: The Fixed Effects of the Liberal Peace," *International Organization* 55, no. No. 2 (Spring, 2001).

Kaplan's nuanced argument centers upon using established local sociocultural and socioeconomic tendencies as a guide for western assistance.[64] He uses Somalia as an example of the failure of western efforts, to fix a fragile state, by force-feeding the Somali people a centralized western-style government.[65] He continues by classifying success as making governments relevant to their populations by using the local, informal, and internally driven political and economic processes imbedded in the society.[66] The development of new approaches for implementing international assistance centers on localizing the help and starting from the existing local structures.

In the case of Somalia, Kaplan highlights the often-ignored Somaliland success story. He calls Somaliland the best democracy on the Horn of Africa and the Arabian Peninsula, in part because of a lack of assistance from the international community.[67] To use Thomas Friedman's term, in *The World Is Flat*, Kaplan champions glocalization of international developmental assistance through the use of existing cultural power sharing systems to achieve stability and chances for a better future.[68] However, the argument for locally grown, distributed, and operated democratic style government, to produce stability, still sounds western. Democratic peace advocates, such as Bruce Russett, view this type of development as keystone for progress.[69]

---

[64] Kaplan., Chapter 1, 8.

[65] Ibid., Chapter 1, 9.

[66] Ibid., Chapter 1, 9.

[67] Ibid., Chapter 8, 1.

[68] Thomas L. Friedman, *The World Is Flat : A Brief History of the Twenty-First Century*, Further updated and expanded ed. (Vancouver: Douglas & McIntyre, 2007). 160-162. Friedman discusses how Wal-Mart created a global supply chain network then tailored the inventory of stores to the local demand. He uses the examples of Wal-Mart stores in China selling live snakes, eels, and pornography, while Florida receives a hurricane season mix of candles, batteries, beer, and board games. Wal-Mart makes the global local: glocalization.

[69] Russett, *Grasping the Democratic Peace : Principles for a Post-Cold War World.*, 30-31. Russett presents, as fact, democracies do not war against each other.

Seth Kaplan calls his version of glocalization an enmeshing of the state within the society.[70] Kaplan views the political, social, economic, and cultural resources of countries in fragile areas, such as Africa, the Middle East, Latin America, and Central Asia, as possessing enormous interactive resources, developed over centuries.[71] He further states that the cultural interactive resources best serve as the blueprint for a functional state government. Kaplan then outlines his principles, or general guidelines, for adapting governance to local conditions. He offers ten steps towards fixing fragile states. Kaplan advocates the following steps: adopt local models, closely integrate state and society, design institutions around identity groups, construct states bottom up, exploit the advantages of regionalism, unify disparate peoples (terrain), supplement state capacity, reinforce and complement local processes, foster private investment and competition, and creatively and gradually increase accountability.[72] Kaplan admits that the ten-step model consists of a major reconceptualization of solutions for fixing fragile states. However, Kaplan discusses four reasons leading to optimism for implementing

First, Kaplan advances that the collective development community advocates a new approach to stabilization of fragile states.[73] Second, he cites the increasing second and third order effects of fragile states such as international security, political instability, humanitarian crisis, human trafficking, and international terrorism. The United States National Security Strategy directly mentions Somalia as an al-Qa'ida safe-haven and at risk for becoming a failed state.[74] Third, Kaplan's new paradigm harmonizes with other initiatives, such as the United Kingdom's Department of International Development nontraditional aid lens approach, to devise an effective means of understanding and remedying state

---

[70] Kaplan. Chapter 4, 1. Kaplan discusses the key to development in fragile states as legitimizing the state by enmeshing it within society.

[71] Ibid., Chapter 4, 1.

[72] Ibid., Chapter 4, 1-13.

[73] Ibid., Chapter 3, 15.

[74] *United States National Security Strategy*2010., 21. The implications of al-Qa'ida in Somalia and the United States National Security Strategy fall beyond the scope of this literature review. However, the monograph will address the importance of Somalia in the United States security policy discourse.

fragility.[75] Kaplan also states that the United States military invested in significant cultural and economic research to help shape operations in Iraq and Afghanistan. He attributed the fall of violence in Iraq during the 2007 timeframe, a direct result of United States efforts to emphasize local institutions and social structures, a template that existed for hundreds of years.[76] Fourth, Kaplan's methods present eminently practicable customization options for local conditions.

Kaplan went on to conduct seven case studies to demonstrate the divergence and congruence of his thesis while bounding the application of his template in terms of duration and intensity. Kaplan recognized that development in fragile states takes both time and effort. Kaplan aims to equip policy makers with better, broad instruments that allow tailor-made policy actions maximum chances to succeed. Kaplan argues that culture dominates human interaction, especially in fragile or failing states, where legacy cultural structures lend toward more effective governance than forced Western mirror imaging. Kaplan's approach appears to suffer Robert Dallek's first myth, that all peoples desire American help.

In contrast, Bronwyn E. Bruton recommends a completely different approach than espoused by Kaplan. Bruton, a 2008-2009 international affairs fellow in residence at the Council on Foreign Relations recommends the United States generally disengage with Somalia, continue precision missile strikes, and deliberately encourage democracy and good governance milestones for regional actors to pursue with Somalia. Bruton's solution looks very different from Kaplan in that she also outlines the fallacies within two alternative policies. She takes issue with continued re-enforcement of the ineffective Transitional

---

[75] Kaplan., Chapter 3, 15. Kaplan uses the British Department of International Development (DFID) drivers of change analysis as an example of harmonizing initiatives to understand state fragility. Kaplan states that the DFID uses nontraditional aid lenses of history, culture, and power dynamics to conduct analysis of fragile countries.

[76] Ibid., Chapter 3, 15. Kaplan cites two newspaper articles from 2007 as evidence that the United States military developed a culturally sensitive approach in Iraq and Afghanistan. Specifically, David Rohde, "Army Enlists Anthropology in War Zones," *New York Times*, October 5, 2005, A1 and Greg Jaffe, "Midlevel Officers Show Enterprise in Iraq," *Wall Street Journal*, December 29, 2007.

Federal Government and offshore military containment of terrorism with missiles and drones.[77] Bronwyn Bruton calls her strategy one of constructive disengagement. The strategy implies that the United States accepts an Islamic government in Somalia, but retains the freedom of maneuver to interdict terrorist threats from Al Shabaab and al-Qa'ida. Bruton dovetails with Kaplan only in using local networks to handle distributing United States foreign aid and anti-piracy operations.

Bronwyn Bruton examines Somalia through a security and a regional lens as a means to outline her recommendations. Somalia primarily concerns the United States for security reasons. She outlines the American fear, post-September 11, 2001, that Somalia could become a major safe haven and staging ground for international terrorism organizations led by al-Qa'ida.[78] Bruton calls American and Western efforts to prevent terrorist safe havens in Somalia as widely counterproductive.[79] She argues that American efforts alienated large parts of the Somali population, polarized the Muslim community into moderate and extremist camps, and thus encouraged discontent with the Transitional Federal Government and the United States. Bruton all but blames the United States, through the Transitional Federal Government, for the rise of Al Shabaab, a radical youth militia from southern Somalia that threatens the survival of the Transitional Federal Government.[80]

The Obama administration expanded on President Bush's policy actions of limited diplomatic and military support for the Transitional Federal Government in hopes of disrupting al-Qa'ida and al Shabaab in Somalia.[81] Secretary of State Clinton observed the Transitional Federal Government as Somalia's best hope for stability, with continued American support to President Sheikh Sharif Sheikh Ahmed. Secretary Clinton's rhetoric, and the current policy, contrast with and appear to support the poor results and track

---

[77] Bronwyn E. Bruton, *Somalia : A New Approach*, Council Special Report (New York: Center for Preventive Action, Council on Foreign Relations, 2010), vii.

[78] Ibid.

[79] Ibid.

[80] Ibid., 3.

[81] Ibid., 3.

record of failed western policy in Somalia. United States support to Somalia comes in the form of ammunition and syndicated diplomatic support messages, along with limited scope non-governmental organization humanitarian efforts.[82] However, Bruton assesses the prospect of the Transitional Federal Government emerging as a viable option for governance in Somalia as unlikely. She cites the Transitional Federal Government's inability to project power beyond a few city blocks in Mogadishu without the assistance from the African Union Mission in Somalia (AMISOM) forces.[83] The Transitional Federal Government failed to consolidate support from the vast majority of Somali clans. Combined with the negative effects of United States and western endorsement, the Transitional Federal Government propelled cooperation among previously fractured extremist groups, many finding a home with al Shabaab.[84]

Bronwyn Bruton argues for a final attempt, by the United States, to help the Transitional Federal Government survive by drawing in the major Islamic clan leaders, including al Shabaab. However, she concedes that the Transitional Federal Government is realistically too weak to endure. Bruton recommends a policy options review for the United States that centers on planning for the disintegration of the Transitional Federal Government while preventing a power grab from al Shabaab. Combating terrorism in Somalia, after a complete failure of the Transitional Federal Government, could prove costly and prolonged, even if a counterinsurgency campaign were feasible. Bruton warns against the diplomatic status quo and one-dimensional limited military actions. American military limited attacks with missiles, drones, and special operations forces only serve to weaken further the Transitional Federal Government's

---

[82] Ibid., 3. Bruton outlines the progression of American interaction with the Transitional Federal Government of Somalia over the last several years. Specifically, she highlights the negative results of the current policy.

[83] Ibid., 3.

[84] Ibid., 4.

image and galvanize opposition groups. Bruton argues that a minimalist counterterrorist campaign, in isolation, would do nothing but compromise Somalia's future even further.[85]

The United States should deliberately lessen direct involvement in Somalia, while undermining al Shabaab and denying al-Qa'ida sanctuary. She recommends a policy of constructive disengagement to achieve reform and progress in Somalia. Bruton's plan details the United States, and other western powers, indicating a withdraw of support for the Transitional Federal Government, while signaling a willingness to support an Islamic government in Somalia.[86] The United States would conditionally provide support to any government willing to refrain from regional aggression, genocide, support to terrorism, global jihad, and agrees to tolerate western humanitarian relief support. With Bruton's recommended path, the United States could consolidate focus and effort to the broader region of East Africa, realize the benefit of allowing Somalia to self select and govern, while enlisting regional and international support organizations to develop new support structures in Somalia.

Bruton identifies three United States strategic interests in Somalia. First, the United States fears that Somalia remains a sanctuary for terrorism. Second, that a complete state failure in Somalia would create a regional humanitarian crisis and potentially destabilize the region. Specifically, a complete collapse of Somalia could lead to a war between clans, Kenya, Eritrea, Ethiopia, and even al-Qa'ida for control of Somalia. Third, the threat of Somali pirates in the Gulf of Aden presents a destabilizing effect on a vital sea-lane of communication in the global commons.[87] Therefore, the primary lens of American interest deals with security.

---

[85] Ibid., 4.

[86] Ibid., 2-5. Bruton spells out her approach through a summary paragraph. She outlines the disengagement, recognition process, and interaction with regional actors as Somalis self-select and regroup for the future.

[87] Ibid., 15. Bruton summarizes her view of American national interest in Somalia.

Somalia, as referenced in the 2010 National Security Strategy represents a terrorist threat to the security of the United States of America.[88] The rise of Somali diaspora fighters and supporters from the United States, increased technical bombing techniques, the Christmas Day bomber, and a public alliance with al Qa'ida in 2010 present the greatest concerns to the United States.[89] American foreign policy makers already support limited military strikes upon terrorist targets in Somalia. Bruton warns against continuing such a limited policy, with out undertaking constructive disengagement with Somalia.

Regional instability, due to Somalia's current situation, also dominates the American policy point of view. Bruton recognizes fragility of Somalia with respect to famine, war, and civil war.[90] A looming humanitarian crisis of wide spread famine, compounded by long standing external conflicts, and a disorganized interior present significant obstacles for stability in Somalia. The northern territories of Somaliland and Puntland also represent a challenge to the authority of the Transitional Federal Government to legitimately govern. The Somaliland people continue a decade long effort to achieve independence and international recognition. The United States continues to recognize the Somali Transitional Federal Government as the only government, but provides some soft support, through anti-piracy and Non-Governmental Organizations to both Somaliland and Puntland.[91] The northern territories represent a possible forcing function for how self-selection and regulation could work in Somalia. If only southern Somalia possessed the ability to follow suit.

Humanitarian concerns, due to instability and lack of governance place many Somalis in a desperate position. Bruton indicates that between one-third and one-half of the population require food

---

[88] Ibid., National Security Strategy, 21.

[89] US, *United States National Security Strategy.*, 15.

[90] Bruton., 16. Bruton discusses the potential for escalation of the Ethiopia-Eritrea conflict into Somalia.

[91] Ibid., 17.

assistance.[92] Since her report, the continued famine in Somalia caused a humanitarian crisis indicated by United States Agency for International Development (USAID) reports and efforts.[93] Continued conflict between al-Shabaab and the Transitional Federal Government, supported by the African Union Mission in Somalia (AMISOM), perpetuate the food delivery problem, as families attempt to flee into Kenya and Ethiopia.[94] In the summer of 2011, Kenya invaded Western Somalia to defeat al-Shabaab elements operating along the border. As the invasion progressed, refugee problems continued to increase as a result of the fighting and famine. Humanitarian efforts by the United States Agency for International Development and the United Nations continue despite the ongoing conflicts.

The United States, European Union, North Atlantic Treaty Organization, and others currently patrol the Gulf of Aden in response to increased high profile piracy attacks emanating from Somalia. According to the International Maritime Bureau, piracy off the coast of Somalia increased from approximately ten attacks in 2006 to thirty-one in 2007 to two hundred fourteen in 2009, capping at two hundred forty-one attacks in 2011.[95] Piracy continues to increase off the coast of Somalia regardless of the number of western naval task force elements operating in the Gulf of Aden.[96]

Bronwyn Bruton sees United States policy responses reduced to three options, which include the continuation of current policy, increased military intervention to support stabilization and reconstruction, and an offshore counterterrorism containment strategy. She warns against all three and recommends another option. Given the realities of Somalia, Bruton recommends constructive disengagement - a

---

[92] Ibid., 18. See United States Agency for International Development, Office of Foreign Disaster Assistance, "Situation Report 9, FY 2009," September 23, 2009. The updated information indicates the recent famine in Somalia as putting two-thirds of the country at risk for starvation.

[93] Ibid.

[94] *Somalia- Complex Emergency, Fact Sheet #2, Fiscal Year (Fy) 2011*2011. Erdogan cites the famine in Somalia this year as the worst in sixty.

[95] Economic Impact of Piracy in the Gulf of Aden on Global Trade, US Department of Transportation, Maritime Administration. December 2, 2010. http://www.marad.dot.gov/documents/HOA_Economic%20Impact%20of%20Piracy.pdf

[96] Recep Tayyi Erdogan, "The Tears of Somalia," *Foreign Policy*, (October 10, 2011)., 18.

containment strategy that would consist of continued counterterrorist operations, increased political and international isolation of al-Shabaab, and actions to minimize regional instability while developing alternatives to Transitional Federal Government and al-Shabaab control of Somalia.[97] Bruton warns that before the Transitional Federal Government collapses, the United States must prepare a new strategy for Somalia.

Conclusion

Security concerns primarily shape the United States policy debate about Somalia. Piracy, humanitarian crises, civil war, and state development move to secondary issues when compared with security and state collapse. American obsession over security, post-September 11, 2001, defines policy narratives towards many states and issues. However, the United States policy towards Somalia indicates that security concerns trump development. Kaplan and Bruton represent two examples of approaches to dealing with legitimate American security concerns in Somalia.

Kaplan and Bruton, provide a picture that represent two prevalent camps in thinking about approaches in United States foreign policy. One camp offers engagement and humanitarian efforts while reforming government actions. The other, offers little in assistance, hedges against regional threats, and maintains the status quo in hopes of a better future. Just as realism and liberalism provide diverging ideas about man, the state, and war, so do Kaplan and Bruton offer vastly different approaches to Somalia.

Within the American illusion of omnipotence and tyranny of metaphor, Walter A. McDougall describes eight American foreign policy traditions as the Old and New Testament portions of the Holy Bible.[98] McDougall labels American foreign policy, post-Cold War, as global meliorism. McDougall's global meliorism is the social, economic, political, and cultural expression of an American need, or

---

[97] Bruton., 18.

[98] Ibid., 10.

mission, to make the world a better place.[99] He bases his argument on the assumption that the United States can, should, and must help other nations share in the American dream. However, this is not always helpful.[100] Again, Dallek and Brogan's tyranny of metaphor and illusion of omnipotence shadow American foreign policy. Joining Robert Dallek and William Brogan, Bronwyn Bruton warns against letting meliorist thought drive complex American foreign policy actions with respect to Somalia. The risks of illusion and metaphor leading the United States towards potential costly misadventures, Dallek style, in Somalia are real.

---

[99] McDougall., 172-173. McDougall describes the eight American foreign policy traditions: Old Testament-exceptionalism, isolationism, Monroe Doctrine, Manifest Destiny, and New Testament- progressive imperialism, Wilsonianism or liberal internationalism, containment, and global meliorism. McDougall outlines each distinct tradition as part of American history, while still relevant to how Americans view themselves and the world. Most important, Americans often Use multiple traditions to explain, justify, or define actions in global politics. (See 208-222 for a summary of the traditions.)

[100] Ibid., 189.

CHAPTER 4

ANALYSIS

Military doctrine and elements of operational art provide tools to describe a theory driven hypothetical approach to implementing policy solutions in Somalia. The Joint Phasing Model allows for points of reference in discussion for implementing operations in time.[101] The Unite States Army operations framework of decisive, shaping, and sustaining provides a method to describe the prioritization of action in the hypothetical.[102] Elements of operational art provide language to synthesize multiple aspects of an operation to meet the intended outcomes.[103] Finally, the feasible, acceptable, and suitable test provides evaluation criteria for contrasting approaches. Military doctrine provides a common language, framework, and lens to examine the possible outcomes of Kaplan and Bruton's approach towards Somalia.

A Kaplan Approach to Somalia: Theory Driven Hypothetical 1

Taking Kaplan's recommendation, a United States intervention in Somalia would change the region permanently. Kaplan's approach starts with the recognition of Somaliland by the United States and international community. A United States led effort to build a coalition of support with in the United Nations for a nation building effort, synchronized with a United States military occupation of the Hargeisa airport and seaport of Somaliland in Berbera. In the first phase of the operation, PH 0 (SHAPING), the United States Government, at the request of the newly recognized Somaliland, provides emergency relief, military assistance, and most importantly, international legitimacy to the Government of Somaliland. The United States Government then provides security assistance forces to assist the

---

[101] Ibid.

[102] *Joint Publication 3-01*1 August 2011. V-6.

[103] *Army Doctrine Publication (Adp) 3-0 Unified Land Operations*10 October 2011. 9-14.

Government of Somaliland to secure its borders. The opening actions represent a pretense for future action.

The SHAPING phase deals with creating favorable conditions within the environment for coalition actions, while developing capability.[104] The actions in this phase provide the groundwork for future operations. During the SHAPING phase, United States and Coalition Special Operations Forces, conduct detailed counterterrorist operations throughout both Somalia and Somaliland. The purpose of counterterrorist operations is to disrupt both al-Shabaab and al-Qa'ida from interfering with the creation of a legitimate Government of Somaliland. Kaplan outlines the strategic importance of Somaliland. Kaplan cites the importance of the Horn of Africa in the Global War on Terrorism, displaying Somaliland as a showcase of democracy and free markets for the region, and providing additional access to the Gulf of Aden for counter-piracy operations.[105]

Seth Kaplan bluntly calls Somalia the "very definition of a failed state."[106] He advocates support for Somaliland, as a forcing function to discredit all Somalia governance, before starting over. Critical to the Kaplan approach is the consolidation of power in Somaliland, to demonstrate to the region and world that a Muslim liberal, secular, democracy can exist. Moreover, establishing a United States friendly nation on the Horn of Africa demonstrates the benefits of accountable, democratic, governance to other Muslim countries.

After SHAPING (PH 0), DETER (PH 1) and SEIZE the INITIATIVE (PH II) follow in the Joint Phasing construct. United States Government and Coalition force transition from PH I to PH II and III

---

[104] Ibid.; US, *Joint Publication 3-0*, II-2 to 6. JP 3-0 defines SHAPING. Shape activities are executed continuously with the intent to enhance international legitimacy and gain multinational cooperation by shaping perceptions and influencing adversaries' and allies' behavior; developing allied and friendly military capabilities for self-defense and multinational operations; improving information exchange and intelligence sharing; providing United States forces with peacetime and contingency access; and mitigating conditions that could lead to a crisis.

[105] US, *Joint Publication 3-0*, V-8. Somaliland: Reconnecting State and Society. Kaplan discusses the security challenges within Somalia and the regional threats.

[106] Kaplan, 2.; http://www.cfr.org/somalia/somalias-terrorist-infestation/p10781. Kaplan uses this Council on Foreign Relations report to call Somalia the "definition of a failed state."

relatively quickly.[107] Most importantly, the United States military forces focus on disrupting terrorist activity in Puntland and Southern Somalia in preparation for peacekeeping and development. The use of military force to eliminate any threat to the Government of Somaliland requires pruning in Somalia while reforming the government structure for the future. Regardless of military operations, the decisive operation focuses on establishing a legitimate government in Somaliland and Somalia with the assistance of African Allies, the United Nations, and other United States Coalition partners.

Kaplan calls Somalia representative of the greatest mismatch between conventional state structures and indigenous institutions among post-colonial countries in Africa.[108] Kaplan posits that clan membership trumps all other forms of civil, social, and political identity.[109] He argues that this fact makes any type of western democracy an instant failure in Somalia. Kaplan claims that only a new form of governance, like in Somaliland, can work in Somalia.

With the collapse of Siyad Barre's socialist government in 1991, warlords and militias took control of Somalia.[110] The warlord structure remained in place until the rise of the Islamic Courts Union in 2006, widely known as a Somali equivalent to the Taliban. Somalia suffered invasions from both Ethiopia (2006) and Kenya (2010).[111] The two invasions, coupled with periodic special operations raids by United States military forces (2003 - 2011) indicate the complete failure of the Transitional Federal Government in Somalia. Kaplan's approach describes Somaliland's success as the rise of an alternative model.

---

[107] Ibid. Phase I defined as actions to deter an adversary from undesirable actions because of friendly capabilities and the will to Use them. Phase II defined as an application of joint combat power to delay, impede, or halt the enemy's initial aggression and to deny the enemy its initial objectives.

[108] US, *Joint Publication 3-0*, V-8.

[109] Kaplan, 2.

[110] Ibid.

[111] Ibid., 5. Journalist Sean Naylor, in a six part series, details the history of American military special and conventional military operations in Somalia and the Horn of Africa.

Kaplan's plan for Somaliland concludes with full United States support to the Somaliland homegrown democracy.[112] He offers that the United States should champion Somaliland as a perfect example of homegrown Muslim democracy for both the Horn of Africa and the Arabian Peninsula.[113] Somaliland, for Kaplan, highlights, as evidence, that leveraging existing cultural institutions eventually leads to sturdy, accountable governing structure.[114] The overall argument against traditional post-colonial development is that western countries tend to disregard the power of existing cultural norms. Specifically, in Somalia, Somaliland is proof that United States and western programs simply do not work when force-fed to the people. Kaplan calls for a reprioritization of inappropriate western development models in Somalia. Democratization and political culture grow best when state institutions represent the fabric of the local culture and reflect the true will of the people.

The military operations described above, indicate a relatively permissive environment with full logistics, security, and facility support from the Government of Somaliland. The decisive operation must establish the Government of Somaliland as both the legitimate and sovereign government. However, the entire operation fails to account for the root problem: Somalia. Recognizing Somaliland reduces the size of Somalia. The true decisive operation must adequately address Somalia. Creating a stable partner with Somaliland provides the United States a perfect platform to project land, sea, and air power directly into Somalia. However, the United States already uses the bases located in Djibouti as the location for Joint Task Force Horn of Africa.

Shaping operations within the Kaplan approach include the United States State Department security sector reform tasks and integrated action across the stability operations lines of effort.[115] The

---

[112] Sean D. Naylor, "The Secret War: How the U.S. Hunted Al Qai'da in Africa," *Army Times* 30 October 2011, Part 1. Kaplan discusses the potential opportunities to shape the African Union and International view of recognizing Somaliland. Specifically, Ethiopia could benefit from a permanently divided Somalia.

[113] Kaplan, 12-15.

[114] Ibid.

[115] Ibid.

Special Operations Command direct action targeting of individual terrorists and networks occurred in

Phase I and continues through the entire operation. The significant shaping operation, in establishing

Somaliland, consists of a deliberate meeting with the ruling clans, warlords, and figures in Somalia. The

United States military and diplomats demonstrate to Somalia a willingness to work towards a new future.

Sustainment operations provide the necessary supplies and equipment necessary for combat operations.

The sustainment required for stability operations focuses directly upon development of host nation

capacity and infrastructure. A portion of the operation includes significant infrastructure development for

Somaliland. An improved infrastructure could develop increased economic activity, access, and

investment for both the international community and Somaliland.

Critique of Fixing Fragile States

Seth Kaplan presents a case study about Somalia in *Fixing Fragile States*. The case study focuses

on Somaliland, not so much on Somalia. As a proponent of development, Kaplan leads off the case study

by highlighting the success of the secessionist northwestern territory of Somalia, or the Republic of

Somaliland. His opening argument calls for the international community to support and recognize the

separatist movement in Somaliland.[116] Strangely, the formal recognition of a separatist province, to

officially establish a new country, cut from the sovereign territory of an existing country, sets a dangerous

international precedent for the United States. Nation building through development is different than

creating nations. In this case, development in Somaliland could serve as a model for all of Somalia.

However, simply recognizing Somaliland sounds like quitting. Regardless, Kaplan sees Somaliland as a

success because the people constructed a set of governing bodies rooted in the traditional Somali concepts

---

[116] *Stability Operations, Field Manual (Fm) 3-0706* October 2008. Figure 2-2, Figure 4-1. Somaliland: Reconnecting State and Society.

of democracy and governance.[117] Kaplan's plan and case study provide little or no actual solutions for greater Somalia. Regardless of international recognition, Somaliland developed a way of life that secures a better future for its people. Somaliland will survive, even if the rest of Somalia continues to produce crisis. Sadly, Kaplan gave up on Somalia as his model fails to deal with the failed state known as Somalia.

Kaplan's approach provides several positive outcomes for Somaliland; however, Somalia remains a failed state. The end state and conditions for success in Somaliland differ from Somalia. Taking an indirect approach to dealing with Somalia helps create a positive generation governance capability elsewhere. A strong Somaliland could encourage the clans in Somalia to reform. However, the phasing and transitions associated with progress in Somalia will look nothing like the tempo of progress in Somaliland. Most importantly, the efforts of the international community, including the United States, culminate in the failure to save Somalia. Intervention equals admission of failure. The strategic risk of attempting to fix Somalia increase as any actor gets closer to the problem. Specifically, the United States must establish Somaliland before continuing to develop the failed state of Somalia.

A Bruton Approach to Somalia: Theory Driven Hypothetical 2

Implementing the Bronwyn Bruton approach in Somalia requires that the United States execute a deliberate disengagement. Bruton calls her approach constructive disengagement. The current policy of supporting the Transitional Federal Government in Somalia is no longer an effective option for stabilizing the country. Bruton argues that the United States signals an agreement to work with an Islamic governing authority in Somalia, regardless of organization. The agreement requires access to Somalia for international humanitarian intervention, denunciation of global Islamic jihad, denial of sanctuary for international terrorist organizations, and limited military access for United States and other forces to

---

[117] Kaplan, 1. The Use of democracy as basis for peace, because of self-selection connects Russett and Kaplan.

conduct counter-terrorist strikes. Bruton warns against planning a military intervention in Somalia, to support the Transitional Federal Government, and continuing offshore containment of terrorist threats and piracy. The Joint Phasing construct, operational framework, and elements of operational art still apply, even for constructive disengagement.

Bruton's approach deliberately reduces United States involvement in Somalia, while disrupting al-Shabaab and denying al-Qaeda sanctuary.[118] Bruton's actions advocate doing less is better than doing harm. Removal of the Transitional Federal Government undermines the marriage of convenience within al-Shabaab. Al-Sabaab neither has the power or cohesiveness to legitimately broker official power within Somalia.[119] By not picking a winner between clans, al-Shabaab, and the Transitional Federal Government, the United States uses disengagement as a forcing function for Somali organization. Bruton expects that a new leadership group or government could emerge. The emergent group would understand the constructive nature of United States and international agreements. The new organization could change the environment if it remained peaceful, rejected global jihad, and facilitated international humanitarian relief.

Constructive disengagement from Somalia requires a United States acceptance of risk. The alternatives of continued military action, radical Islamic entrenchment, al-Qa'ida sanctuary, and a forever-failed state are far worse. American policy makers would begin by this approach by signaling a withdrawal of support from the Transitional Federal Government. A United States led effort to coordinate support for making a change in Somalia must come from the African Union, Intergovernmental Authority on Development, and the United Nations mission in the African Union Mission to Somalia.[120] The

---

[118] Ibid.; Russett, *Grasping the Democratic Peace : Principles for a Post-Cold War World*, 99-103.

[119] Bruton, 3-5.

[120] AMISOM. African Union Mission in Somalia is the named operation created by the United States, approved in the United Nations for assistance to the Somali people after the failure of both the Ethiopian invasion and TFG in 2009. See http://amisom-au.org/about/amisom-background/ for background information from AMISOM about the mission in Somalia.

peaceful dissolution of the Transitional Federal Government requires support and assurances from clan leaders, including al-Shabaab. Securing an agreement to peacefully dissolve the Transitional Federal Government and establish a dialogue with clan, warlord, and al-Shabaab leaders represents the decisive portion of Bruton's approach.

Shaping the environment for possible negotiations with an emergent government would consist of continued United States Special Operations forces raids and counterterrorist operations. Shaping activities critical to the constructive disengagement policy involve international access for humanitarian assistance, limited anti-piracy operations, development without regard to form of governance, as well as increased international and regional partner diplomatic efforts.[121] The United States must guarantee stability for the fledgling government by keeping both Kenya and Ethiopia from invading Somalia. The buffer concept works internal to Somalia. The United States would open higher-level diplomatic access to both Somaliland and Puntland in an effort to establish United States Agency for International Development offices. With access, the United States also establishes port operations to Somaliland and Puntland as a sign of goodwill and to encourage al-Shabaab to become a legitimate alternative.[122]

Bruton's approach requires significant diplomatic effort, strategic messaging, and yet small military involvement beyond contingency planning and direct action counterterrorist efforts. The largest portion of the strategy involves acceptance of the Somali people in self-selecting an Islamic government. Key to the Bruton approach is the ability of the international community to monitor and guide Somalia, while shifting focus to Kenya, Ethiopia, Eritrea, and Djibouti.

Bronwyn Bruton recommends an indirect approach to dealing with Somalia. A planner would require extensive line of effort planning to coordinate unity of effort among the interagency team for implementation of Bruton's plan. However, the operational sustainment and reach requirements remain

---

[121] Bruton, 5.

[122] Ibid., 23-35.

miniscule. The United States could consider placing a sizeable reserve in Djibouti as a contingency to provide the threat of joint military intervention. Regardless, the risk associated with Bruton's approach lies in the United States admission of failure in fixing Somalia since 1991. According to Bruton, the risk far outweighs the alternative narratives unfolding in Somalia.[123]

Critique of Constructive Disengagement

Bronwyn Bruton's constructive disengagement provides an excellent argument for pulling back from Somalia, with continued limited United States military options, to allow a localized governing solution to emerge. She offers objective criticism of two popular concepts of off shore containment and full military intervention.[124] Taken at face value, the approach seems to fit the zeitgeist of shifting focus to Asia and the Pacific, while withdrawing from Iraq and Afghanistan in a budget-constrained environment.[125] However, leaving an entire country under the potential control of a non-state actor, terrorist organization, like al-Shabaab, only invites the next potential 9/11 type of attack. Strategic risk of a new terrorist sanctuary and the possibility of an al-Shabaab, the al-Qa'ida affiliate, coordinating a massive terrorist strike against the west create issues for Bruton's approach.

Portions of both Kaplan and Bruton's approach take shape in examining counter-piracy operations within the current operational environment. The United States conducts counter-piracy operations off the coast of Somalia with participation in several naval task forces. Given an understanding about the international relations theory, two current approaches (Kaplan and Bruton), and two theory driven hypotheticals one can understand the complexities of conducting counter-piracy operations in the

---

[123] Ibid., 31-33.

[124] Ibid., 35.

[125] *The American Heritage Dictionary of the English Language*, 5th ed. (Boston: Houghton Mifflin Harcourt, 2011). Zeitgeist means the spirit of the times; the taste and outlook characteristic of a period or generation.

Gulf of Aden. The above analysis provides insight to the problems facing Somalia that examining counter piracy operations clearly illuminate.

Conclusions and Recommendations

The United States foreign policy approach for dealing with Somalia, and Eastern Africa, requires a customized set of actions. Defeating al-Qa'ida and al-Shabaab in Somalia remain the top priority. The Obama Administration, as stated in the 2010 National Security Strategy, continues to view Somalia as a safe haven for terrorism and therefore, policy will most likely remain fixed around counter-terrorism. However, terrorism, as explained in this paper, is simply a symptom. The United States should continue efforts to destroy al-Qa'ida and al-Shabaab while executing a deliberate constructive disengagement program recommended by Bronwyn Bruton. The United States should claim a neutral position in support of any emergent governance system in Somalia. The theme of Somali self-selection must dominate the dialogue.

The United States can focus United States Agency for International Development current efforts without regard to the flavor of governance. International assistance, in the form of Non-Governmental Organizations can play a significant role in helping reduce the effects of state failure. When implementing constructive disengagement, Non-Governmental Organizations should lead humanitarian efforts while conflict in Somalia stabilizes. The United States should reduce development funding and allow form to follow function, as Somali created organizations emerge.

As United States direct efforts reduce in Somalia, United States support to Kenya, Ethiopia, Eritrea, and Djibouti increase. Continued long-term development in these countries can lead to increased access to the region, and Somalia. Seth Kaplan's recommendations for a nuanced policy perfectly apply to re-examining the focus of American development in Kenya, Ethiopia, Eritrea, and Djibouti. The indirect pressure of invigorated assistance to East Africa could serve as powerful motivation for stability in Somalia.

The United States should develop a roadmap to international recognition for Somaliland. The opening of direct negotiations with Somaliland through the United Nations and the African Union sends a powerful message to the warlords and clan leaders in southern Somalia. The recognition of Somaliland carries precedent from the recent creation of Southern Sudan. Moreover, the United States can assist the new Somaliland government and procure additional influence in the Horn of Africa.

BIBLIOGRAPHY

The American Heritage Dictionary of the English Language. 5th ed. Boston: Houghton Mifflin Harcourt, 2011.

Brogan, William. "The Illusion of American Omnipotence." *Harper's Magazine*December 1952.

Bruce Russett, John R. Oneal, David R. Davis. "The Third Leg of the Kantian Tripod for Peace: International Organizations and Militarized Disputes, 1950-1985." *International Organization* 52, no. No. 3 (Summer, 1998): 441-467.

Bruton, Bronwyn E. *Somalia : A New Approach* Council Special Report. New York: Center for Preventive Action, Council on Foreign Relations, 2010.

Burton, Bronwyn. "Disengaging from Somalia, Interview by Deborah Jerome." *Council on Foreign Relations*, (March 10, 2010).

Coggins, Bridget. "The Pirate Den." *Foreign Policy*, no. July/August (2010).

Dallek, Robert. "The Tyranny of Metaphor." *Foreign Policy* 182, (2010).

Dolman, Everett C. *Pure Strategy : Power and Principle in the Space and Information Age* Cass Series--Strategy and History. London ; New York: Frank Cass, 2005.

Erdogan, Recep Tayyi. "The Tears of Somalia." *Foreign Policy*, (October 10, 2011).

Friedman, Thomas L. *The World Is Flat : A Brief History of the Twenty-First Century*. Further updated and expanded ed. Vancouver: Douglas & McIntyre, 2007.

Gaddis, John Lewis. *The Landscape of History : How Historians Map the Past*. Oxford ; New York: Oxford University Press, 2002.

_____. *Surprise, Security, and the American Experience* Joanna Jackson Goldman Memorial Lecture on American Civilization and Government. Cambridge, MA: Harvard University Press, 2004.

Kaplan, Seth D. *Fixing Fragile States : A New Paradigm for Development*. Westport, Conn.: Praeger Security International, 2008.

Kegley, Charles W., and Shannon Lindsey Blanton. *World Politics : Trend and Transformation*. 12th ed. Australia ; Boston: Wadsworth Cengage Learning, 2010.

Kreisler, Harry. "Theory and International Politcs: Conversation with Kenneth N. Waltz." (February 10, 2003).

Lynn, John A. *Battle : A History of Combat and Culture*. Rev. and updated ed. Cambridge, MA: Westview Press, 2004.

McDougall, Walter A. *Promised Land, Crusader State : The American Encounter with the World since 1776*. Boston: Houghton Mifflin, 1997.

Mearsheimer, John J. *The Tragedy of Great Power Politics*. New York: Norton, 2001.

Naylor, Sean D. "The Secret War: How the U.S. Hunted Al Qai'da in Africa." *Army Times* 30 October 2011.

Nietzsche, Friedrich Wilhelm. *Human, All Too Human : A Book for Free Spirits*. Lincoln: University of Nebraska Press, 1984.

Nye, Joseph S. *Soft Power : The Means to Success in World Politics*. 1st ed. New York: Public Affairs, 2004.

————. *Understanding International Conflicts : An Introduction to Theory and History*. 7th ed. Longman Classics in Political Science. New York: Pearson Longman, 2009.

————. "Get Smart." *Foreign Affairs* 88, no. 4 (Jul/Aug 2009): 5.

Nye, Joseph S., David Welch, and Joseph S. Nye. *Understanding Global Conflict and Cooperation : An Introduction to Theory and History*. 8th ed. Boston: Pearson Longman, 2011.

Peace, Fund For. 2012. "The Failed State Index," http://www.fundforpeace.org/global/?q=fsi-grid2008.

Pham, Peter J. . "Lawyers Vs. Pirates." *Foreign Policy*, (April 30, 2010).

Ploch, Lauren. *Piracy Off the Horn of Africa* September 28, 2009.

Russett, Bruce M. *Grasping the Democratic Peace : Principles for a Post-Cold War World*. Princeton, N.J.: Princeton University Press, 1993.

Russett, Bruce M., and John R. Oneal. *Triangulating Peace : Democracy, Interdependence, and International Organizations*. New York: Norton, 2001.

Russett, John R. Oneal and Bruce. "Clear and Clean: The Fixed Effects of the Liberal Peace." *International Organization* 55, no. No. 2 (Spring, 2001): 469-485.

Schouten, P. "Theory Talk #40: Kenneth Waltz- the Physiocrat of Internatinal Politcs'." *Theory Talks*, (2011).

Thucydides. *The Landmark Thucydides : A Comprehensive Guide to the Peloponnesian War*. Newly rev. ed. New York: Simon & Schuster, 1998.

United Nations, Security Council. *Report to the Secretary-General Pursuant to Security Council Resolution 1897 (2009)*, October 27, 2010.

US, Agency for International Development,, Bureau for Democracy, Conflict, and Humanitarian Assistance (DCHA). *Somalia- Complex Emergency, Fact Sheet #2, Fiscal Year (Fy) 2011*, 2011.

US, Department of the Army. *Army Doctrine Publication (Adp) 3-0 Unified Land Operations*, 10 October 2011.

_____. *Stability Operations, Field Manual (Fm) 3-07*, 06 October 2008.

US, Department of Transportation, Maritime Administration. *Economic Impact of Piracy in the Gulf of Aden on Global Trade*, December 02, 2010.

_____. *Countering Piracy Off the Coast of Africa: Partnership Action Plan*, December 2008.

US, Joint Forces Command. *Joint Publication 3-0*, 11 August 2011.

US, Office of the President *United States National Security Strategy*, 2010.

Wade, Geoff. *The Polity of Yelang and the Origin of the Name "China"*. Vol. No. 188 Sino-Platonic Papers.

Waltz, Kenneth Neal. *Man, the State, and War; a Theoretical Analysis* Topical Studies in International Relations. New York,: Columbia University Press, 1959.

_____. *Theory of International Politics* Addison-Wesley Series in Political Science. Reading, Mass.: Addison-Wesley Pub. Co., 1979.